Agent Allies reads like a masterclass in Marketing. Ramsey redefines ROI, describes powerful partnering, and devotes an entire chapter to event mastery. I thought Agent Allies was going to be a book to recommend to lenders, warranty reps, and real estate allied services, but what I discovered is that Agent Allies will be referred to anyone who needs to understand that every business is a media company in today's economy."

—Michael J. Maher, CEO of REFERCO, Bestselling author of (7L) The Seven Levels of Communication and Miracle Morning for Real Estate Agents, and Founder of the Generosity Generation

"Remington Ramsey hits the mark with Agent Allies. It's the ultimate guide to mastering sales, marketing, and mindset in the real estate world."

—Justin Donald, #1 WSJ and USA Today Best-Selling Author, Founder of The Lifestyle Investor, Host of The Lifestyle Investor Podcast

"This is the book you didn't know you needed. Agent Allies will give you the tools to build relationships and close deals with agents."

—Chandler Bolt, CEO of SelfPublishing.com

"Agent Allies is a must-read for anyone working with agents. Remington Ramsey offers real, practical advice to thrive in the real estate world, delivered with wit and wisdom."

—Wayne Salmans, CEO of Hero Nation Coaching

AGENT ALLIES

**BUILDING YOUR BUSINESS WITH STRATEGIC
REAL ESTATE PARTNERSHIPS**

REMINGTON RAMSEY

Agent Allies: Build Your Business Through Strategic Real Estate Partnerships
© Copyright <<2024>> Remington Ramsey

All rights reserved. No part of this publication may be reproduced, distributed or transmitted in any form or by any means, including photocopying, recording, or other electronic or mechanical methods, without the prior written permission of the publisher, except in the case of brief quotations embodied in critical reviews and certain other noncommercial uses permitted by copyright law.

Although the author and publisher have made every effort to ensure that the information in this book was correct at press time, the author and publisher do not assume and hereby disclaim any liability to any party for any loss, damage, or disruption caused by errors or omissions, whether such errors or omissions result from negligence, accident, or any other cause.

Adherence to all applicable laws and regulations, including international, federal, state and local governing professional licensing, business practices, advertising, and all other aspects of doing business in the US, Canada or any other jurisdiction is the sole responsibility of the reader and consumer.

Neither the author nor the publisher assumes any responsibility or liability whatsoever on behalf of the consumer or reader of this material. Any perceived slight of any individual or organization is purely unintentional.

The resources in this book are provided for informational purposes only and should not be used to replace the specialized training and professional judgment of a health care or mental health care professional.

Neither the author nor the publisher can be held responsible for the use of the information provided within this book. Please always consult a trained professional before making any decision regarding treatment of yourself or others.

For more information, visit remingtonramsey.com.

ISBN Paperback: 979-8-89316-468-8
ISBN Hardback: 979-8-89316-467-1

GET YOUR FREE GIFT!

I have found that *Belief* is one of the strongest indicators of successful people and I wrote a short ebook to help with mindset on belief. Visit remingtonramsey.com to download your free copy today:

You can get a copy by visiting:
remingtonramsey.com

ABOUT THE AUTHOR

Remington Ramsey is an innovative entrepreneur and the mastermind behind *Real Producers* magazine, a nationwide platform boasting over 140 locations. He combines his experience in real estate and passion for storytelling to empower both agents and vendors. Based in Indianapolis with his wife and four children, Remington is dedicated to fostering collaboration and connection in the industry, helping others unlock their full potential in the real estate world.

ACKNOWLEDGEMENTS

To my amazing wife Kelsey and our four incredible kids. You guys are my MVPs. Kels, I thank God for you every day and for keeping our house from total chaos while we pursue our dreams together.

To my parents, Dr. Brian and Tammy Ramsey—thanks for raising me to be a man of faith and for always pushing me to aim higher. And Dad, thanks for jumping in to help outline the book and kickstart the writing process. I'm pretty sure this thing wouldn't exist without you.

To Duane Hixon and Earl Seals—thank you for betting on a young, wild entrepreneur and joining me on the journey to build Real Producers. You didn't just make my dream a reality, you've helped shape what's become something far bigger than I ever imagined. Appreciate you pushing me to always level up.

And to the RP franchise owners, you are the heartbeat of Real Producers. You're not just distributing magazines—you're literally changing the game, one issue at a time, connecting and telling the stories of the real estate industry in a way it's never seen before. Thank you for leading the charge!

AUTHOR'S NOTE

When I first named this book *Agent Allies*, my initial thought was that the title referred to agents being the allies that help vendors build their businesses. But later, I realized it could also be interpreted the other way around—that we, as vendors, are the allies helping agents succeed. The truth is, both are correct.

The real estate agent is at the center of the real estate world, but the vendors who support them are just as crucial in keeping that world turning. Whether you're an agent or a vendor, this book is written with you in mind. We're all in this together. Except for appraisers. What's up with those guys?

CONTENTS

Introduction – Why did I write this book? 1

SECTION I: TRANSFORMATION: CHANGING YOUR MINDSET

Chapter 1: ROI: What Does it Actually Mean? 11
Chapter 2: Becoming One With Your Brand 21
Chapter 3: Overcoming Obstacles: A Story Actually Worth Sharing..27

SECTION II: IMPLEMENTATION: BUILDING YOUR BUSINESS WITH PARTNERS

Chapter 4: Storytelling: Master the Art 39
Chapter 5: Go for Silver...49
Chapter 6: Event Mastery: The Bar Is Set Low....................................67
Chapter 7: The Star of Your Show: Rethinking Your Marketing.......................77

SECTION III: THINKING BIGGER

Chapter 8:   The Greatest Salesman in the World..........85
Chapter 9:   Becoming Recession-Proof........................91
Chapter 10: It's All About the Story..............................99

Pay It Forward...105

INTRODUCTION

WHY DID I WRITE THIS BOOK?

At the start of my journey in real estate, I was handed the book by Gary Keller and Jay Papasan that everyone is supposed to read on day one: *The Millionaire Real Estate Agent*. I thought, *But I'm not a real estate agent*. And that was true; I was a vendor. But I was encouraged to read the book to better understand the way agents think and act *and* learn a thing or two about selling. Over the years, I found myself wishing someone wrote the same book from the vendor's perspective. And then it hit me. *Why isn't that person me?*

I built one business around solely calling on real estate agents, then I spent the next 10 years building a brand that coached vendors on how to call on real estate agents while offering a service that produced events and a magazine. That brand is now in 140-plus markets and known as *Real Producers* magazine. This book is a window to my journey and a how-to guide for anyone who is looking to build their business as a vendor in real estate.

I made my entrance to the real estate world the same way most people do: by selling knives. That's not how you entered? Maybe it was a bit unconventional. Yes, I was that kid who called your mom and sold her knives and then asked for the names of all her friends and family so that I could then change *their* lives with my knives. After many years of building a book of business in residential knife sales, I decided to take my talents to a specialty division called CUTCO Closing Gifts. It had quickly become the largest closing gift company in the country, which was really only rivaled by gift cards and gift baskets.

I enjoyed the real estate side of things for two reasons. One, I enjoyed working in a more business-to-business (B2B) climate where I was working with other business owners also looking to grow. The second was the residual aspect of gift sales. When real estate agents ran out of gifts, they needed to buy more. And then they would call me—if I had done a good job of earning and retaining their business. The challenge was identifying which real estate agents were actually selling enough homes to afford my gifts and then earning their business long-term.

I turned to the process that was the go-to for most vendors: buying donuts, bagels, and various bread products and bringing them to the sales meetings to earn a few minutes at the beginning of my dog and pony show. Don't get me wrong, I got pretty good at that. My rule was that if I could get the real estate agents to laugh three times in the five minutes given to me, then I had earned their trust and intrigued them enough to get a one-on-one, which meant the sales ratio was close to 90 percent. Because, as we all know, the *top* real estate agents love going to sales meetings.

Kidding aside, that presented another major challenge: the sales meetings were typically geared toward newer agents, and companies struggled to get their top-tier agents to consistently attend…which meant I also suffered.

Additionally, I would attend the bigger events, where I would set up a booth for typically $500 to $1,000, which was a lot for a poor, struggling knife salesman. I remember stamping the cards of real estate agents who would visit my booth, but just wanted a full card so they could enter the drawing at the end of the event. Most of the time, a small percentage of the event was the vendor show, and the majority involved the big hall that housed their awards ceremony and continuing education (CE) classes. I distinctly remember sitting there and staring at the other vendors for hours on end, waiting for the next break when a real estate agent might trickle in and wander over to my booth. The struggle was real.

Even on my lunches, I would make vital mistakes. Turns out, just because real estate agents say they are number one in the city on social media, it doesn't mean they actually are. WHAT?? *Did you know people lie on Facebook?* I would take them out for fine dining and spend $100 on lunch to impress them, only to find out they sold a grand total of two homes the year before—but they sure did love the shrimp cocktail at St. Elmo's!

> **SIDENOTE**: The National Association of REALTORS© (NAR) came out with a stat that said two out of three real estate agents that launched with a license that year would not be in the business the following year. Real estate is the largest trade organization in the world. It also has one of the largest turnover rates, if not *the* largest. At that given time, there were 6,000 real estate agents on the board in Indianapolis, and *half* of them would sell one or fewer homes that year. You read that right.

I decided that while I loved donating my time and money to the cause, it was time to create a new process that would weed out the part-time agents and bring the movers and shakers to the table so that I could work smarter, not harder. It started with events.

Instead of spending tens of thousands a year on each individual brand and brokerage, I created my own events. I remember the first event like it was yesterday. It was a month before Thanksgiving, so I had the wild idea of giving away turkeys to see if there would be a turnout. We called it Turkey Time. The turnout blew my mind. Not only did I have my clientele show up, but they also brought friends who were agents, all of whom were actually selling homes. What normally took me an entire week to sell took me two hours, *and* they were new sales in addition to repeat business. I was also able to get the food and venue covered by two other vendors who thought I was onto something. Light bulb! If I could get the right real estate agents to show up and engage, other vendors would want to participate and even pay to do so. Pay attention, Remington.

That was just the start. Every quarter afterward, I was bringing a new client appreciation event to the table. It was actually really fun coming up with creative themes, activities, and prizes.

The next step was creating the newsletter. My initial idea was to take a top client of mine and make them the "real estate agents of the month," then send out a digital newsletter including their recognition. The concept was there, but the execution, not so much. First off, I learned long ago that I am not an artist by any means of the word. I need to stay in my lane. But at the time, I had no staff and was doing everything myself, which is what all great business books suggest. *Eye roll.*

That's when the idea for the magazine hit. I have always said I want to think bigger than everyone else. I don't want to win a Guinness World Record; I want to be Guinness. I don't want to be on the cover of a magazine; I want to own the magazine. This was a chance to put it all together. It will never *not* be cool to be on the cover of a magazine.

"*But Remington, print is dead.*" Doesn't matter.

"*But Remington, people have tried and failed.*" Doesn't matter.

"*But Remington, real estate agents won't care to read about other real estate agents.*" Not true. But also, it doesn't matter.

I ended up meeting with over 50 real estate professionals to run my idea by them. Many had great insights and a handful believed, but almost all of them told me it probably wouldn't work, or they just simply told me not to do it.

Even after all that, there was never a moment when I didn't believe *Real Producers* was going to happen in a big way.

After locking in the dream, it was time to team up with a national company to make it happen. The N2 Company made the dream a reality. Having already specialized in niche products and magazines, they were about to surpass 100 million in annual revenue and operated in virtually every market that I envisioned *Real Producers* thriving in. The two owners of N2, Duane and Earl (sounds like the hosts of a fishing podcast), were eager to add on new products that could further the brand and reach more people and markets. Shortly after, *Real Producers* was born.

Since the beginning, we've focused on a few key ingredients that set *Real Producers* apart from every other real estate magazine:

1. It is sent for *free* directly to the top real estate agent in every market, sorted by volume of business.
2. We host events for the top agents and their teams a few times per year, when we highlight their stories and give them a chance to rub elbows with the best in the industry.
3. We strengthen the community by connecting the top real estate agents with the best service providers in the community and connect them with like-minded real estate agents who will make their deals run smoother.
4. We provide third-party validation for their businesses so they can show their sphere how successful they are without the hard sell.

AGENT ALLIES

Over time, we have expanded our focus to include two more important areas. The first is recruiting the best of the best to bring this movement to over 150 communities nationwide. It takes a very unique individual to do all the things we ask of this brand and its people.

The second is positioning myself and everyone under the RP brand as a coach to vendors who want to build their business around the best real estate agent in town. I believe we have tapped into the very best way to do so, and the book you are about to dive into is a compilation of everything I have learned in the last 15 years while building a business around real estate professionals. They're a rare breed, but one that I have come to love. My hope for you is that in the pages to follow, you find a simple step-by-step process on how to take a business to the greatest heights of success using essential principles that I have discovered.

So take a break from calling 100 real estate agents a day.

Put your credit card back in your purse, and put the bagels down.

Learn to say no to the next broker who just needs to get their party paid for. Yeah, *I said it*. True value needs to come from all participating parties. From the time I put down the chef knife and started printing the magazine, people have always asked me, "So, Remington, how did this come about? How did you build your business?"

So I would tell them, not just about my story and my path, but how I believed they could take a similar one.

And then they would say, "You should write a book."

This is the book.

Agent Allies isn't just the story of my path to the top. It's a guide on how you can take a similar path and find more success calling on real estate agents to build your business.

Disclaimer:

You may have read a book like this before. You may have heard many of the principles discussed in these chapters. But growth junkies love to hear it again. Growth junkies ask themselves if they are applying it and living it. Growth junkies ask themselves, "*Am I doing this so well that I could write the book?*"

I've heard the "*you are the average of the five people you spend the most time with*" message at least 100 times. But every time, I stop and ask myself, "*Who are the top five in my life right now?*" It may have changed since the last time I heard it.

No one says, "I've already seen a movie before." *This* movie is different.

"I've already eaten food before." Sure, but most doctors recommend eating daily.

Who's hungry?

TRANSFORMATION: CHANGING YOUR MINDSET

CHAPTER 1

ROI: WHAT DOES IT ACTUALLY MEAN?

I remember my first day selling advertising like it was yesterday. I was so sure of my products, yet so unsure of how to handle the most basic objections. Remember, most people knew me as the closing gift guy. They knew I had grown a decent business calling on agents but entrusting me with their marketing dollars was a different conversation altogether.

> Prospect: Hey Remington, can you tell me the ROI?
> Remington: Sure. Right after you tell me what ROI stands for. (By the way, it's a *return on investment*, for those of you who were as lost as I was.)

Not only was I unsure how to answer that, I didn't even have basic stats on my product, as the division did not exist. The brand did not exist…yet.

However, I knew the product was going to work, and everyone who was involved was going to win. That was enough for me to get it off the ground. I was able to sell a quarter of a million dollars in pre print sales simply because the concept was so strong. There was never a time when I didn't believe in *Real Producers*, so my goal was to share that same passion with every vendor I came in contact with.

It occurred to me that the ROI objection was keeping great companies from joining this great movement, and it was not because I did not have a good answer for ROI. It was because they didn't.

They had a bad perspective on how to judge and evaluate ROI. Most people think about ROI and marketing in the same breath. The unfortunate demise of that line of thinking kept others from making important moves that would make their businesses and personal brands stand the test of time. Consider space engineers: they never think their calculations are "*close enough.*" If that rocket is a few feet off in trajectory, it will miss the target. I want you to be "*dead-on.*"

Most of the time, people boil ROI down to "How much money do I give you?" and then, "How much will I make from the money I gave you?" The difficulty with this line of thinking is that it is impossible to quantify the results from the marketing decisions that people make in a timely manner.

This takes time. Marketing takes time. I have never gone into a coaching call where the person on the other end said, "I really want to build this for a year, and then I am going to quit and do something else."

My father worked in several state prisons in central Indiana for five years as a director of education. I asked him once why the prisons were full. Note that the common response from most people boils down to lack of fathers, poverty, and a few other ideas. But he told me that the college faculty believed that the lack of education was the number one reason why people went to prison and stayed in prison. He believed that education could be the one thing that would get them out and offer them a chance at a productive life.

In that same vein, we are in a prison with our thinking and our marketing dollars. Every person I have ever met who has "*marketing*" in their title believes ROI should be a number they can track. The only thing that is going to get us out of that prison and into the world of strong branding and marketing is educating ourselves on the *why's* and the *how's* of doing it the right way.

We need to educate ourselves on where to spend our money and our time effectively. If we are going to judge the true ROI of our investment in marketing and branding, there must be a proper definition of what this principle is and how to apply it.

I have a new acronym that I think is more appropriate for ROI:

R: Reach

O: Optimal

I: Impact

Ask yourself these key questions:

Reach: How many eyeballs are seeing this? What platforms are we using? This is a quantitative analysis.

Optimal: Are they the right eyeballs to have the best opportunity for success? Are they qualified or next-level prospects? At *Real Producers* magazine, we use the top 500 agents—not all ten thousand agents that sell in our area.

Impact: Does it make you feel something? This is the "eye" test—or in this case, the "I" test. We can use the example of social media for this one. Are we too focused on likes? Are we overly focused on the comments? Consistency leads to impact and value. Divorce yourself from the immediate results and note that you are providing value and service, and therefore you are making connections with people. That is the true impact of your marketing.

The Jeep Wave

The best way I can explain this concept of ROI is by giving examples of some powerful brands and strong products. Consider the Jeep Wrangler. When I bought a Jeep Wrangler, I realized after a short time that it was the most social car on the road. Everyone was waving at me. The cool people made a peace sign, and the coolest people lifted a few fingers up from the wheel and never even looked at you. I thought, *That is who I want to be when I grow up.*

After my purchase, my mind was rewired to see Jeeps everywhere. The truth of the matter is that the Jeeps were always there, but I just started *seeing* they were there. Honestly, it does not matter what car it is. It is the same for everything from a Prius to a GMC pickup truck.

I Drank Way Too Much Coke

I want you to consider one of the strongest brands of the last 50 years: Coca-Cola. The fact that Coke is still constantly advertising everywhere should tell you something. I used to drink a ton of Coca-Cola. While growing up and in college, I drank way more than I care to admit, but when I was in my mid-twenties, I had a strong realization that I probably should not be drinking that much. I made a radical change and cut the habit from my diet, though occasionally, I will still have a Coca-Cola.

I always wonder on those days, why did I finally break down and have a Coke? I ponder how many billboards I must have seen with Coca-Cola on them, or how many commercials, or if there were advertisements I wasn't even aware of in the break room. Was there a Coke vending machine, or was someone drinking one and I could smell it? Maybe I heard the "pop-fizz" when they opened it. It was a compilation of all those things that made me finally break down and drink the Coke.

Fairway Mortgage and Golf Carts

I assumed every real estate agent had a big hot air balloon logo and way too much hairspray. These are the people that sell houses. I pronounced the word REALTOR "real-la-ter" and referred to the act of selling a home as "flipping a home," regardless of how it was being sold. I had no idea what I was doing, and I had no idea what Fairway Mortgage was.

Fairway Mortgage was the lender that we used to buy our first home, and the lender did a good job. I remembered his logo from his golf polo. The next day, I was golfing at one of my favorite courses and saw that Fairway Mortgage logo on the golf carts. *That is just crazy*, I thought.

So, I called my lender, teasing him, saying, "You are stalking me. One day I am closing a house, and the next day you are advertising at my favorite golf course."

He replied, "Remington, I have been advertising on those golf carts for two years."

That was a light bulb moment for me. I had probably seen that sign a dozen times, but until I had an association with it, including the name and logo of the brand, I had never really seen it. And that is what branding really is.

Picture this scenario with me and my Fairway Mortgage loan officer:

I met Eric at a party. Cool. I do not need to buy a house.
I notice Fairway Mortgage on the logo on his T-shirt. I still do not need a house.
I bump into Eric at church—still no house.

I see Eric and Fairway Mortgage at a real estate event. I do not need anything.

I get online and see an email from Eric. I do not need to buy a house.

I see a post from Eric on Facebook—not even thinking of houses.

A year passes, and now I need to buy a house. Whom do I choose? You guessed it! Obviously, I choose Eric. He has been there all along to bring it home (pun intended.)

Again, you make an investment to be everywhere the "*eyeballs*" are. You do it for months and even years, sometimes before someone says they notice it, but when they are invested, those ads solidify themselves in the minds of your sphere.

The next generation is obsessed with personal brands, as they should be. *Selling ourselves is the number one thing that will never go out of style.* I believe loyalty and brand recognition is a good way to build a personal brand.

When I was selling CUTCO knives, I hustled hard to be known as the "CUTCO guy." At first, it was a little embarrassing, but the money fixed all of that. After that, I wore the "knife guy" title as a badge of honor. It progressed to the point that I loved seeing CUTCO advertisements everywhere, even if I was not the rep in the ad. I knew I was hustling so hard that regardless of who was in the ad, the second my peers and clients saw the brand, they would immediately think of me.

If you are one with your brand, much like Eric was, that can only be a good thing for you. People will start to see your loyalty to that brand. They will associate you with that established brand and see how hard you hustle—even to the point that they want to do business with you and partner with you, even on other ventures, activities, or events. What if you decided to start a side hustle? The loyalty to your brand will help you launch the side hustle, no doubt.

So back to Remington selling advertising. I quickly figured out that it wasn't a paper ad I was selling. I was selling access. I was building a community and selling access to the strong vendors who did business the right way. My favorite response was when people told me they only do word-of-mouth advertising, to which I replied, "Great! We weed out the agents that waste your time and bring the top agents into a space where they see and talk about you on a regular basis." As I told you before, I never lacked the confidence that this program was going to take off. The magazine and events were just the beginning.

I'm not trying to tell you how to do it as much as tell you how I did it. Later on, I am going to show you my process for turning a single client into many and building your circle, but understanding the true ROI on my time and money was essential. When I let go of making sure every dollar I spent on events and marketing came back to me in a week, it allowed me to breathe and do what I do best: *build relationships.*

Chapter Takeaways:

1. If Coke still advertises without knowing its true ROI, maybe you should relax.
2. Reach as many eyeballs as you can.
3. Optimize and target your top-tier prospects.
4. Impact: Make sure you are branding in a way that reflects your message and provokes the viewer to take action.

CHAPTER 2

BECOMING ONE WITH YOUR BRAND

While I was building my business brand in closing gifts, I realized that I was also building a personal brand at the same exact time. I realized my personal brand was also acquiring *Agent Allies* when I began receiving this response:: "*Whatever you are doing, we want to be a part of it.*" This contributed to the early success of Real Producers in Indianapolis.

Those words meant so much to me. I heard them from vendors and real estate agents alike and I'm willing to bet that many in the industry fail to realize how important a strong personal brand is in the process of building a book of business. Why is that?

Personal branding has grown to be one of the biggest buzzwords on social media, and it's confusing our loyalties.

Is it possible to be a "company man" but also build your personal brand? Can I represent a company well while also building my own personal following and loyalty? I believe the two should be simultaneous, and if done correctly, everyone wins.

Let's back up…

This issue starts earlier than you think.

Kids these days no longer want to be cowboys and princesses. Their number one ambition in life is to be a YouTuber and make millions before they hit their teenage years. The problem with this concept is the ratio for success. For every one social media influencer, there are thousands of wannabes on the outside looking in. What actually happens when you only dream of success is you wind up living in your parents' basement watching YouTube videos instead of creating the ones that get you to heightened success.

From millennials to Gen Z, we see this trend in real estate. The average first-time homebuyer age is getting older and older because they are still stuck in their parents' basements. They romanticize the success and don't realize the luck that comes to those child-star YouTubers.

When I was selling CUTCO knives, I was totally cool with people calling me the CUTCO kid. It gave me pride knowing that people thought of me that way, that I was doing a good job, and that I was a company man. I was one with the brand. I loved hearing all the kids who were a few years younger than me coming into the office saying, "I didn't make a sale because they said they already work with Remington." It happened all the time.

I learned how to hone my skills in sales and how to run a business. Originally, the magazine was just a side hustle to sell more knives. At some point, the side hustle took over. This route meant the magazine wasn't a massive undertaking that I took on with no income, like you see in the movies. It doesn't have to be that drastic. It makes for a good rags-to-riches story, but again, that's the one out of 100 who makes it. I would rather build my business after having learned the skills from being in the industry first.

Instead of becoming another statistic, I applied a technique that is duplicatable and provides income and stability along the way.

Step one: Identify a field you are interested in *and* find a job you don't hate. This is harder than it sounds. Know how I know? One of the most popular phrases in our society is "Thank God it's Friday." Why is that? Because the weekend is when the highlight of our lives happens. How could work be a highlight? Work is laborious and exhausting. I work to get paid so I can have fun on the weekend.

Flip that script. Most of the people in my sphere can't wait to get working on Monday after a nice chill weekend. Find a job that makes you say, "Thank God it's Monday," for starters.

Step two: Develop skills that will help you. The number one skill you need to develop is how to sell, hands down. The most challenging, and arguably most important, pillar to building a business is the sales pipeline. Learn how to sell that product like a beast. Even if you will ultimately leave to do your own thing, you will likely be selling the same or a very similar product to the same group of people, which works nicely alongside step three.

Step three: Develop connections that will help you. Never dismiss people in your industry. You never know how they could become a great ally in the game. Show your loyalty to the brand you are currently with. Make recruiters jealous that they don't have a hustler like you in their midst. People are drawn to the hustle. They want to be a part of it and they will want to be a part of your next venture when the time comes.

**For anyone reading this who has no desire to run their own business, disregard steps four and five. However, simply applying steps one through three will not only help you grow, but it will also help you become so valuable that job security will never be an issue. But if you do have that entrepreneurial itch and think to yourself, *Maybe I would like to work for myself,* check out the last two steps.

Step four (optional): Start the side hustle. Gary V. is one of the greatest examples of this. He was the manager at his parents' liquor store and was passionate about wine. So he started an extremely low-budget YouTube show called *Wine Library TV* and learned how to sell wine on the internet. He got so good at it that he started advising others on how to scale a business on the internet, and now he is known as one of the greatest social media influencers of all time. He is a tycoon in the social media space and started as the *Wine Library* guy.

Step five (optional): Become an entrepreneur. Now, you don't have to go off on your own. Maybe you enjoy working with another business. If you are truly "*one with* *your brand,"* then it's possible you will always be a diehard and have no desire to leave. That's great! Many spend their lives in pursuit of a job where they feel appreciated and fulfilled.

But if not, when the time is right, make a big splash into entrepreneurship. If this is your path, make sure you self-educate. Books, mentors, and "YouTube University" will be your biggest advisors.

PRO TIP: Wait until your side hustle is bringing in enough cash to sustain a modest lifestyle before making the transition. Then you know that you can survive, and growth will only impact luxuries.

Embracing your current brand will always yield positive results. People are drawn to loyalty. They will notice how hard you work for a brand that you are proud of, and other opportunities will come your way. When I first started running sales appointments to build the magazine, I heard on multiple occasions, *"Remington, honestly, I trust you and want to be a part of whatever you are doing. I'm in."*

Chapter Takeaways:

1. Books, audiobooks, podcasts, and videos are readily available to educate oneself on virtually any topic.
2. Don't wait for your dreams to come true. Start working in the industry to gain skills and connections.
3. Develop a side hustle and be okay with the progress. It's a side hustle. No rush.

CHAPTER 3

OVERCOMING OBSTACLES: A STORY ACTUALLY WORTH SHARING

When creating *Real Producers* magazine in 2015, I had to overcome one big obstacle: "Print is dead." I heard that phrase more times than you can imagine. What does that even mean?

Is it like when they say Latin is a dead language? But we kind of still use Latin. So it's only *mostly* dead, like the line in *The Princess Bride*. Got it.

"*Remington, print is dead.*" That was the mountain to climb, the obstacle to overcome if I was going to realize this dream.

Obstacles are a funny thing. I find that most people try to avoid them. My good friend Bobby Wright launched the second *Real Producers* franchise in Columbus, Ohio. Bobby and I talk often and we are constantly looking for the lesson in every scenario…especially obstacles.

Recently, he was explaining to me why his favorite animal is the African water buffalo. When a devastating storm hits, most animals run from the storm and prolong the amount of time they experience it. The water buffalo walks into the storm in order to get through it faster. That is the mindset you must have to attack obstacles head on.

There are two additional things you have to keep in mind before addressing obstacles: 1) Do you believe your product or service is the solution to a problem, and 2) does your faith outweigh the doubt of others? If so, it really doesn't matter what the obstacle is. The foundation is there for you to overcome virtually anything in your path. Then you just rinse and repeat.

Do you believe your product or service is the solution to a problem?

The problem in my situation was that real estate agents were not showing up to real estate events. As vendors, we could not get in front of them in the conventional ways. Sometimes, agents do not even show up to their own sales meetings. Not the "real producers," anyway. What was the solution? For us, it was creating a community where the agents were incentivized and excited to attend the events.

After that process, we still had the roadblock of that phrase, "Print is dead." But print was not, in fact, dead. In reality, print was very much alive in niche products. My rule on content was we would not print things anyone could "google," which was exactly what most print mediums failed to realize. Print was not dead; the majority of the content that was being printed was dead—or in this case, oversaturated.

AGENT ALLIES

Think about a local newspaper. Why would I continue to read a local newspaper when I could get the same news quicker from my phone, text my friends, and play Candy Crush while consuming that news?

Answer: I wouldn't. At the end of 2023, *The New York Times* had 10.36 million subscribers, 9.7 million of them digital-only.

The key to keeping print alive was printing things that you could only find within that medium. So, the magazine became "*Facebook-in-print*" for a select community, which happened to be the elite few within real estate. Thus, the two answers to the objection were first, printing material that can only be found within the magazine, and second, making sure it was elite and exclusive. Only a small group of people have earned the right to even receive this magazine, and that strategy created quite the buzz.

I believe. Do you believe?

One of the greatest obstacles in business and in life is our own limiting beliefs. Limiting beliefs typically happen because of something in your past. Example: You were in an accident, so you avoid that road, fearing it might happen again. When we come across limiting beliefs, we have to intentionally address them so that we do not prevent ourselves from reaching success.

Have you ever been to the circus? You have probably seen elephants that weigh over 16,000 pounds and could literally tear down the tent and run away at any time. Yet, they stay in place and never leave. These strong, massive animals are trained to believe that they are not capable of breaking the chains. When a baby elephant is born, trainers will tie their legs to a stake in the ground so they cannot move. After hours of trying to get away from the stake, the baby elephant simply gives up. That is all it takes to make the elephant think that anytime they feel the pressure or the resistance, there is no point trying because there is no escape. The elephant's belief is not rooted in truth, but they believe it.

Here are a few of the limiting beliefs or "what ifs" that would creep into my head while we were ramping up Indy *Real Producers* and franchises to follow:

- What if people don't renew?
- What if the excitement wears off?
- What if I run out of real estate agents?
- What if people stop coming to events?
- Will this really make a difference?

What causes us to get into this place? Maybe a bad renewal cycle leads us to believe that nobody renews. Maybe a client yelled at me on my last call, and now I believe that every client is mad at me when I speak to them. Maybe I had a bad showing at an event, so now I believe that every time I throw an event, I will struggle to get attendance.

It was in these moments that I had to work backward to ensure that my beliefs were rooted in truth. I walked myself through the following dialogue on a daily basis until it was ingrained within me:

Do real estate agents still sell homes? *Yes.*
Is it hard to reach them? *Yes.*
Is there a need to connect real estate
    agents with vendors? *Yes.*

Are there niche magazines that people
    still love to read? Yes.
Do I have the backing of a 100-million-dollar
    publishing
    company? Yes.
Have I created events that agents show up to? Yes.
Do I play "Eye of the Tiger" every
    time I get into my car? Yes.
Can I bring all of this together? Yes.
Doubt eliminated. Put your head down
    and work, Remington.

Have you ever been in the zone and selling the same thing over and over? You think, That is the package everyone wants. But really it's the one that you have found yourself selling because you are comfortable selling it.

The value YOU have for your product or service will become your ceiling. In other words, if you sell a service consistently for $500, we can assume that you don't think your service is worth much more than $500, even though the company average for that service is $1,000, or twice as much.

When coaching our publishers, we have created the term "quarter page queen" or "quarter page king" for someone who sells the cheapest thing we offer over and over again. It happens to be the quarter page. Cute little ring to it, right?

The reason they are selling the cheapest thing over and over really boils down to the value they have for the service. They believe *Real Producers* is great but only worth X amount. I like to do a little drill with them and ask,

"What would you purchase if you were a lender/title company/home inspector?"

Most of the time, they answer with a half or full page but can't articulate why. So the next step is to list out all the reasons why someone would buy a full page:

1. Bigger ads are more eye-catching, and they stand out.
2. They have an ad size that communicates they mean business with the top real estate agents.
3. Bigger ads and premium spots get them to the top of the list for hosting events.
4. One single client they earn pays for three years' worth of advertising.
5. It's a better bang for the buck, etc.

After putting themselves in the shoes of the client, they decide it's worth spending more, and they experience a breakthrough in their next sales cycle.

The beauty of sales is that it ultimately rests in your hands. That's a great position to be in. When it's not going the way you want, *you* are the answer. And it is a lot more exciting when *you* are the reason it is going so well.

No pain, no gain.

Obstacles are things that can define us, regardless of the outcome, by the way we react to them. You might have heard the saying "Life is 10 percent what happens to you and 90 percent how you respond." For example, you could say, "*My parents were alcoholics, and that is why I grew up to be a homeless alcoholic myself.*" Or you could say, "*My parents were alcoholics, and that is why I grew up being intentional about recovery from addiction and loving toward my children, since my parents were not there.*" In both cases, the parents were alcoholics. That is the 10 percent. The 90 percent of the rest of your life was dictated by how you chose to handle each event or circumstance.

There is a lecture taught by Dr. Abraham Twerski in which he talks about lobsters, and it is one of the best images of overcoming obstacles that I have ever heard. He talks about lobsters being these soft, mushy animals that have a hard outer shell, and in time, the lobster grows and is confined by the shell. For it to continue growing, it must go behind a rock, shed the shell, and then produce a new shell that it can then grow into.

The catalyst for growth is discomfort, and he talks about the fact that if lobsters had doctors, they would never grow. They would just be prescribed a pill for the pain, and they would never shed their shell. Thus, they would never be able to grow. For us, we need to realize that the catalyst for growth is sometimes captured in the most painful obstacles of our journey.

If we decide to go through obstacles and learn from them, we will grow infinitely more than if we run away and do not address them. I am glad that I did not believe everyone when they said print was dead. I am glad that my faith in the program outweighed the doubt of those who said agents would never show up. Ten years after my start, we are now in 150 markets and still growing. There are very few places you could visit where the real estate agents do not know the name *Real Producers*.

Real-life example

When the pandemic happened in 2020, it was one of the greatest displays of "giving in to circumstances" that the world has ever witnessed. Some people, quite simply, did not go back to work because they were collecting paychecks to stay at home. Labor forces could not attract labor. Work did not get done. There was even a shortage of chickens because there was no one to farm the chickens.

We had a front-row seat and witnessed two schools of thought: 1) I could use this to my advantage and become a lower-class citizen, and 2) I can get ahead by doubling down my efforts in a world where no one else seems to be paying attention.

I decided that sitting around and collecting a paycheck I did not earn was not an option. Instead, my inner circle looked for the opportunity of the moment.

There was a pizza franchise near my office building that failed two times over the course of six years. My friends and I used to eat lunch there, and when it went under, we wondered who would take it over. Then the pandemic hit and took a serious toll on the food and beverage industry and the people who worked in that arena. Restaurants were shutting down left and right. Light bulb. We made the decision to get into the industry and leased the location when everyone else was leaving. Within one year of negotiating the lease, our doors were open, and the world met Parks Place Pub.

Fast-forward three years and we have been voted the "Best Sports Bar in Indianapolis" by Fox59. We have gained quite the following of regulars and have dozens of staffers who have been with us since the beginning. All of this happened because we were paying attention and decided to do something uncommon. The year 2020, despite its challenges, could quite possibly be the reason we became successful.

Chapter Takeaways:

1. Overcoming obstacles boils down to belief and action. Does your faith outweigh others' doubts?
2. Can you identify limiting beliefs you have developed that may be affecting your results?
3. Work backward and write down everything that is true about your future success.
4. Look for the opportunities amid the pain. Obstacles can be the very things that propel you into success.

SECTION II

IMPLEMENTATION: BUILDING YOUR BUSINESS WITH PARTNERS

CHAPTER 4

STORYTELLING: MASTER THE ART

We all tell stories...some better than others.

I want you to think of your favorite movie for a second. Now think of your favorite book—besides this one, of course. What does your favorite movie and book have in common? Among other things, I am guessing it's the story or even the way the story is told.

My favorites have always been the rags-to-riches stories. Think *Rudy*. There are some movies that appear on television, and even though we own them on Amazon, Apple TV, and DVD, we still decide to watch them. As I am channel surfing, there is *Rudy*, and I think, *Welp, I guess I know what I am doing for the next two hours.*

What makes *Rudy* a great story?

Immediately, we are pulled into the scene of a family that loves their football. They, like us, work really hard, and one of their shared joys is Notre Dame football. We see their commitment, but what slowly emerges is the dream Rudy has to play at this school. We are slowly drawn to adopt his dream, and as the story progresses, we feel his pain and wait with eagerness when each admissions letter comes, only to be crushed—one more year of junior college. He makes it, though, and the final scene of the game where Rudy enters and makes the tackle has us cheering as we wipe our tears and celebrate the joy of making it up the mountain of perseverance. Epic storytelling for a movie. (Especially if you know the real story. But that's a tale for a different time.)

In this chapter, I want to show you why storytelling is essential in all areas of your business, but especially in marketing. Then, I will show you examples of how to do this "for real life," like my six-year-old always says.

Think about the core of what we do at *Real Producers* magazine: we tell stories. It sounds simple, but the strategy behind it makes all the difference. We feature our agents by simply telling their stories. The partners we sign on—we are telling their stories. However, if all we did was share the story behind why the business was successful, few people would read it.

When we originally started, we had a business side and a personal side to the magazine. As we progressed, we realized that there were so many business resources out there, and what made us different was telling the unique stories behind the people who were successful in real estate. The most successful marketing strategy is sharing compelling personal stories.

Bailey and Wood

Mike Wood is the owner of one of the most successful mortgage companies in Indiana. He called me up one day to invite me to his annual event. Mike's explanation of the event was so passionate that I could not even comprehend what it was all about. His passion moved me to buy a ticket but I was still unsure of what I would be walking into. So, I arrived, found a seat, and then tried to get my bearings. I was sitting among a crowd of over five hundred people. I had no idea of the magnitude of this event. Why were they all there?

Most of the people in attendance came to the event expecting good food and people to speak with, but they were not going to be involved in the program. The real estate agents who were present would not be receiving anything. There were no awards or recognition for them. I'm expecting a gasp from the real estate agent reading this. *What do you mean they didn't give real estate agent awards? That is the only reason I show up for our sales rally.*

Kidding aside, all these people literally came to watch loan officers receive awards from the owner of the company. The mere ability he possessed to get over five hundred people to attend demonstrates the culture he created.

Mike took the microphone and began to share the story of the humble beginnings of his company. When he decided that he was going to start his own business, he had very little money, but he did have a big heart and a lofty vision. He proceeded to develop the story, and I could see him drawing the entire crowd into this scenario. I could tell it was not being told for any effect; it was just the sincere expression of his story.

Continuing, he described the finishing touches to the creation of his company, and at the end, he had to turn in some paperwork to make it all official. In all the pressure of trying to get everything completed, the clerk pointed out that Mike had not put down anything for the name of the company. He slowly looked down into the eyes of his seven-year-old daughter standing next to him, realizing that the entire company was present for this momentous occasion—the two of them: Mike Wood and his daughter, Bailey. With tearful eyes, Mike said to her, "Well, it is just you and me." He looked up at the clerk and said, "Bailey and Wood."

As I looked over the crowd of more than five hundred people, I could have heard a pin drop. Everyone resonated with the fact that during the next twenty years or more, his success would never overshadow these humble beginnings. He would never forget, and neither would we.

When he was telling that story, I could feel the emotion of the moment, almost like from the movies. It was as if his emotions were mine. I was standing next to Bailey. I was Mike looking down at Bailey. You had better believe I teared up with Mike. I connected with his personal story, and yet it also connected me to his business indirectly.

Back to my original question. Why did so many people show up? They wanted to see the next chapter.

Now, maybe you are reading this and you are thinking, I do not have a story that big or contains that much emotion. You might think, I wish I had some really cool details surrounding my business that would make people identify with my struggles.

Maybe you are a private person, and you do not want to share your own story or reveal any of the details of your struggles or roadblocks.

I have some great news for you. Mike's story is compelling and emotionally heartfelt, but sometimes all you need is a story that gets straight to the pain point of the listener. Sometimes, an even more effective means of storytelling is actually making the client or prospect the star of your show and the centerpiece of your story.

Fairy-Tale Endings

We love the fairy-tale, feel-good endings to stories, do we not? Rudy finally makes the team and gets in the game as a senior, and while being carried off the field, the crowd chants his name—fairy-tale ending. Frodo returns the ring to Mordor and restores peace to Middle Earth—fairy-tale ending. Harry and Lloyd finally return the briefcase to Mary Swanson—fairy-tale ending.

If you add the fairy-tale ending feature in business, you will master the art of storytelling in marketing. Let me give you an example using a vendor. Consider a junk removal company. Here is an example of a great ad in which they are telling a story:

> Imagine cleaning out your basement to meet a deadline to list your house. You had no idea there would be this much junk, and

you just need to pitch it. The real estate agent has set a timeline that you agreed upon, and you really want to hit the market on Thursday. Now, your entire garage and even your driveway are packed with crap (pardon my language).

You know that you could haul it in your brother's truck, but he is out of town all of a sudden. He does that from time to time. What should you do? Call me, the junk removal guy. Give me an hour and I will be there—with friends.

Now that is an example of great marketing and storytelling. This really beats the alternatives that we all see a lot:

We haul junk for $100 an hour.

or

We remove large and small items.

You can see how the first example tells the story and puts the prospect into a position and mindset where they really feel the pain of the situation and they know the solution is this junk removal vendor.

Here is a second example. What if a lender were to write a social media post that looked like this?

AGENT ALLIES

> Everything was smooth sailing. You were pre-approved, and you had a great relationship with your lender. They seemed sharp and knew a lot of big words that you did not know. So, clearly, you are glad you hired this professional, but as it gets closer to the closing date, he keeps asking for more documents. These new documents seem like they are putting him in a panic. "I thought we were all good," you remark. "Are we going to get the loan now?" He assures you everything is fine and that the underwriter just does this sometimes. But you have been burned before. Now you are worried, and it is ten days away. Then seven days away. You cannot even reach this guy. Now what is going on?
>
> Does that sound familiar? Give us a shot, and I promise we will be upfront and give you 100 percent of the facts every step of the way. Not only that, we have products that most do not have access to, and we will get the job done.

Put yourself in the shoes of someone reading that and compare it with the lender who posts this to social media:

> We do FHA, VA, Conventional, LMNOP, blah blah blah…

or even

We close on time.

That is a good start, but what if you had that story before those words, "We close on time"?

Getting Your Story Out There

So, those are two examples of how to effectively tell stories that will help market your business. Now, what we must do after we have constructed our stories is figure out the platforms on which we will tell them. If we are talking about marketing dollars and time spent, it's important to carefully consider each.

Here are four of the strongest platforms I have found to communicate your stories:

1. **Email**. Contrary to popular belief, email marketing is alive and well. If you are a junk removal company, you can literally copy and paste that first scenario into an email and send it out to your list along with a meme. Go ahead, add it to your drip campaign.
2. **Direct mail**. A picture is worth a thousand words. Show a solid picture with a person pulling out their hair and a junk pile a mile high behind them. "What do I do?"
3. **Storytelling in person**. This happens on your personal visits or even in your elevator speeches.

"Yup, just bailed out another person drowning in junk at the last minute. It's my life. It's what I do. And I love every minute."
4. **Social media** is the obvious medium, though it is important to know how each one works and how it performs differently from the others.

Since the inception of social media, the strongest platforms have been the following:

- Facebook
- YouTube
- Instagram
- LinkedIn
- X (Twitter)

Do you have a plan for each one? Here is a checklist for making your posts more effective:

1. Use humor. Have fun with it.
2. Post memes that resonate with you.
3. Use strong pictures that tell a story without needing words.
4. Define these things:
    a. *Why* is always the first question you define. Is this ad in tune with your ultimate why?
    b. *Who* is this written for?
    c. *What* is the goal?
    d. *When* is the ideal time to have this hit eyeballs?
    e. *Where* are the best places to share this story?
    f. *How* do we capitalize once the ad is out?

5. Follow other pages that do what you want to do and emulate them.

Again, what makes *Rudy* such a great story involves several features or tools. There is pain—a lot of pain. We feel the pain. We want so badly for Rudy to succeed. Everyone is telling him to quit. He continues. We see his rise and then the final test. He almost quits but doesn't, and in the end, we celebrate the happy ending that is only as strong as what he triumphed over.

Are you telling the story of triumph in your marketing? Are you letting us feel the emotion in the story? Are we struggling alongside Rudy? Do you have the triumphant solution that provides us with that fairy-tale ending? If you do, we will continue to watch it every time it pops up on television—or in a magazine, for that matter. Over and over again.

Chapter Takeaways:

1. Storytelling is essential to any brand campaign.
2. Create a plan around telling the story of your clients' pain.
3. Address the different mediums of advertising and how your story will be told on each platform.
4. Have fun. Life is short.

CHAPTER 5

GO FOR SILVER

In this chapter, we're going to talk about how to win clients and how to get your current clients to use you more. And then a third, and probably most important, point is how to get your current clients to multiply.

Step one, get a client.

Step two, get the client to use you more frequently.

Step three, turn that client into multiple clients.

Step One, Get a Client.

This is going to sound like I'm oversimplifying it, but I can tell you after ten years of directly coaching hundreds of business owners that the single most important thing for you to do to get an initial client is to be in the room. Be in the room? What room? What does that even mean?

There are many rooms, but ultimately, I'm talking about the rooms that real estate agents are in. You need to go where the agents are going. And not just any agents, the ones who are actually doing the business. You've heard me describe going to events that only the new real estate agents who couldn't afford my products and services attended. We need to go to the events where the top producers are the movers and shakers.

On top of that, we need to be in the rooms that they are in on social media. That is where you bring it all home. It's a cheat code. You bring all the rooms to you at once, and you multiply yourself. The reason why it's important to simply be in the room is because when someone is looking to make a change, convenience in this culture is put at a premium.

Be everywhere. I tell my franchisees often that it is more important to be in the room than it is to be good at your job. Landing the deal, at times, is as simple as being seen more than the other guy. Once you get the first deal, how you perform will dictate repeat business. However, the single greatest compliment you can receive is the phrase "*I see you everywhere.*" Then you know your hustle is working.

Think about how often you've ordered food instead of getting off your butt and going to get it yourself. Think about using a credit card instead of cash, even though you know a 3 percent charge is going to be added to it. Think about all the decisions you make simply because they will save you five seconds, like typing "lol" or "BRB." We place so much importance on convenience. Even when making big business decisions, the second someone doesn't want to use a vendor any longer for any reason, the first person they think of is the one who's been alongside them, calling on

AGENT ALLIES

them, who is actually simply in the room at that time, and it's convenient to then give them that business immediately.

Once we have landed that first client, we have completed step one.

Step Two, Get the Client to Use You More Frequently.

This is where you need to nail the customer experience. It's six times cheaper to market to your clients than to find new ones. They use you more, and they refer their friends for incentive. A good activity to do for your business is to organize your clients into categories.

To start, here's a statistic that you should remember when establishing a business calling on real estate agents: two out of three agents that train and get their license this year will not be here this time next year. It is a revolving door. Real estate is the largest trade organization in the world, and it also has the highest turnover rate.

When we redo the distribution list once a year for *Real Producers*, anywhere between 30 and 40 percent of the list is new compared to the year before. What does this mean? It means real estate agents get better. They retire, they leave, or they merge. And because real estate is a revolving door and there's so much turnover and change within the top agents, this is good for you. This means you need to be establishing your business around real estate agent that are stable and have been for the last 10 to 20 years but also adding the new real estate agent, the up-and-comers that are going to be here for the next 10 to 20 years, so that you have a healthy balance of both.

Your first category will be your gold group. These clients are not necessarily the real estate agents that sell the most. You can use them for marketing. Here's what I mean.

If a real estate agent is doing $100 million worth of business but they've only used you two or three times, that means they're not giving you most of their business. Whereas a real estate agent who's doing $5 million but gives you all of their business is actually financially better for you. Both can be part of your gold group, depending on how you look at it. If you're defining your top group based on how much time, money, and effort you're spending on them because of what they can gain you, even that top real estate agents who's not giving you a ton of business can be valuable to you because you can tell others that the top real estate agents that makes over $100 million uses you.

So your gold group is made up of two types of agents: the agents that are top real estate agents that you can use for promotion, and the other agents who may not be quite as established in sales but give you a ton of business over and over again.

The second will be your silver group. Silver is anyone who has ever used you, even one time. Silver is where we are going to live for this chapter. We are going to go for silvers. And here's why: The bronze group simply consists of prospects. Just for stepping into the game of real estate, I am giving you a bronze medal. Welcome to the game (or in this case, hunt.)

Here's the breakdown:

Gold Group:

- Successful, well-known agents that have used you before. You can use them for marketing and promoting to other agents. This lets them know you are the real deal simply because the top dogs choose to use you.
- Agents that use you frequently. These agents are reliable, and you don't have to put in as much effort to win their business over and over. You have a good relationship. (It may be easier to love on them because you know them well and feel a sense of gratitude.)

Silver Group:

- Agents who have used you one or more times but don't have quite enough volume to be in the gold group. Maybe they don't have a big name or they are at the beginning stages of testing the waters with your relationship.
- My entire strategy for building a book of business revolved around my outlook on silvers. How can I make more bronzes into silvers? And more silvers into gold?

Bronze Group:

- Anyone who dares step into the real estate arena. Having just decided to get their real estate license, they have entered the thunderdome of your marketing and networking. Look out, rookie.

Most people spend most of their time, money, and effort on the bronze group, going out and getting more real estate agents to use them just one time, getting their name out in front of people who've never seen them before, and living in those rooms. The problem with that is what we said before: it's six times more expensive to go out and get new clients than it is to actually advertise to your current database. The reason we're going to live with the silvers is because everyone who's ever used you at least one time has already been through the most difficult conversion, which is the first-time use. Provided you did a great job on that deal, they should be inclined to use you again.

Step Three, Turn That Client into Multiple Clients.

But when you start to advertise to them, that's when it gets fun, because they send you their friends who also want your awesome services. Clearly define your silvers and make a plan of attack to grow your business. (Simple Graphic: This is where we create a graph to move silvers into golds and bronzes into silvers.) Here's something to know as you start to grow:

- The **top 20** percent love you and will always use you.

- The **bottom 20** percent will never use you no matter what you do for whatever reason.
- The **middle 60** percent is where you should live.

These are the ones that just need some encouragement to use you at least one time. The biggest mistake I see people making is spending all their time, money, and effort on gold and bronze. They're either hanging out with people who use them all the time or they're spending time in completely new rooms and disregarding the biggest group of people, the silver group. Stay in front of your silvers. When I first started selling closing gifts with CUTCO, it was hard for me to crack the code on most brokerages. They had heard it all before: "I only want five minutes." "I can bring donuts." "Everyone loves me." But they were skeptical.

They were especially skeptical of a kid selling knives who didn't own a home and had no business teaching real estate agents about anything. But one smaller brokerage gave me a shot. And the majority of my clients in that first six months came from that brokerage. In time, some of the larger brokerages had clients that became more valuable for a few reasons. Number one, they bought more. Number two, they referred more. And number three, they were influential in their office and brand, so I could use them in marketing. Up-and-comers, or rising stars, are fun because they haven't decided who they are using eternally. They aren't jaded from the years of business, and they will keep getting better and remember who helped them along the way. Now you have staples mixed with newbies, and these two lists will grow.

Remember that not all real estate agents are created equal. NAR says that 49 percent of all real estate agents will sell one home or less in a calendar year. So what do we do with this information? Do we need to spend all of our marketing dollars on the bronze group? "There are a lot more real estate agents that do *not* use me than *do* use me. Maybe I should spend money there." But then you find out that many on that list can't afford you because they don't sell much. It changes the game. And it makes silvers that much more valuable. Because silvers hang out with other silvers.

I'll say it again. It's six times cheaper to advertise to your current database than to go out and get new clients!

One group we often overlook in all of this is the affiliates themselves. Making a strong connection with someone on the vendor side can reap big benefits. Whose circles are you in? Are you a goal group member? For some, that's one of the quickest ways to naturally build their own circle. Are you a good client?

We've all heard of the industries that are annoyed by real estate agents. They don't want to call on real estate agents because agents waste their time or they're super bossy and just want to get the job done, blah blah blah. The real estate agents that "get it" take care of their vendor partners. When someone moves into a home and they need to know who to call on for a dentist, where to eat, or what to do on the weekends, the real estate agent is the first person they call. So if the real estate agent wants to be the one-stop shop, they better take care of their vendors.

Take Jason the painter, for instance. Jason has a backlog of three weeks before he can even start a project. But you need something done in the next three days. Well, if you have a good relationship with Jason, guess what he's going to do for you? He's going to move mountains to make it happen for you. I'm guessing that he wouldn't do it for another real estate agent who simply doesn't return calls. So if you're a real estate agent and you're reading this, don't treat vendors like second-rate citizens. They truly are your partners. They, quite literally, could be the person who gets the deal done faster simply because you took care of them and took their call.

I interviewed my friend Jason, the painter from above, for this book to do a deep dive into his business and see what we can learn about his clients. Here are the answers to his questions:

CASE STUDY: Jason with Heritage Painting

Jason with Heritage Painting has taken his business from humble beginnings to impressive heights. Back in 2012, they were pulling in a modest $350K, but fast forward to 2023, and they've hit $4.8 million, with their eyes set on $6.2 million in 2024. Not bad for a company that started with a few paintbrushes and a dream. Heritage Painting now boasts a team of 15 management staff and operates with a hybrid crew of internal painters and vendor partners. It's safe to say they've come a long way from simply picking paint colors.

Marketing has been the secret sauce behind their success (besides the perfect paint finish, of course). Their main marketing expenses include a monthly newsletter—yes, the old-school, snail-mail variety—along with targeted postcards and an impressive online presence, especially on Google. These three marketing pillars have been the bread and butter of their growth. And because no one can resist rubbing elbows at a good event, advertising in *Real Producers* magazine and attending industry events have also become key parts of their strategy. Turns out, networking isn't just for cocktail parties—it's also for painters who know how to market like pros.

Luckily, most of their marketing tasks are now systemized, meaning they can focus on painting walls instead of painting themselves into a corner with endless marketing duties. Strategic partnerships with vendors, real estate agents, and paint suppliers keep the business flowing, and their business coach keeps them sharp. They're also active members of the PCA and APPC—because it's always a good idea to have friends in high places.

After reading *Giftology*, Heritage Painting embraced the art of strategic gifting, which has certainly paid off. Their typical clients are dual-income households with a $150K+ income, who'd much rather hand over a paintbrush than use one. And who can blame them? The average spend per project is around $5,200, and once clients experience Heritage's handiwork, they're likely to come back for more. Plus, with over 950 Google reviews, it's clear these guys know their way around a roller—and customer satisfaction.

One of their key strategies is partnering with real estate agents, and here's the kicker: every client who refers to Heritage Painting is helping not just their business, but the agent's as well. Jason's philosophy is simple: "You refer us, we build our business, and we'll do everything we can to help build yours too." It's the ultimate win-win—plus, it never hurts to have a few painters in your back pocket, especially when you're a real estate agent looking to seal the deal on a freshly painted home.

Beyond these foundational strategies, Jason has introduced several next-level implementations to further solidify his brand presence. For instance, he leaves stickers on paint cans that clients store in their garages, ensuring his contact information is readily available when they need to match paint colors. He also stays on top of market trends, ready to revamp his brand as needed, and practices grassroots marketing by handing out business cards to drive-through workers, creating potential future connections. He encourages these workers to contact him if they ever want to work for a good company, and they might pass his card along to others.

In 2018, Jason's business reached $1.7 million in revenue with a modest $12,000 ad spend, largely reliant on his visibility and personal efforts. As his business grew, he increased his ad spend tenfold, though the revenue did not increase at the same rate. Faced with this challenge, Jason is now considering whether to push further with his current strategies or pivot to new ones.

Marketing experts often suggest spending 6 to 12 percent of revenue on marketing efforts. Reflecting on his first year, when he generated $350,000 in revenue and now *spends* that amount annually on advertising with a revenue of over $4.8 million, Jason's 12 years of growth demonstrate significant progress. The success of his strategies has been so promising that he is now working on franchising his business model, aiming to replicate his achievements on a larger scale.

I can tell you firsthand as one of Jason's clients that he applies the "Go for Silver" approach. He reaches out to me often through many different channels, and I have been thrilled with the work he has done for me and every person we have recommended to him. He has turned me, a single silver, into many other silvers, so much so that I will most likely be promoted to gold status before long… at least, I hope. I need a good discount on an upcoming exterior paint job!

Dream 100 List

We've focused on silvers for much of this chapter, so I want to close with my process for prospects that I hoped to turn gold. I sent out a Dream 100 letter to 100 different real estate agents that I aspired to work with. I got this idea from *The Ultimate Sales Machine* by Chet Holmes. Many of our top reps gave out this letter with a single closing gift, and it worked. I didn't close all of them that way. But the ones I did more than made up for the money spent on all the gifts.

Here's an example of what the Dream 100 letter looks like:

Dear Tracy,

Your sales and leadership in the industry have landed you on my Dream 100 List. You are someone I know I can learn from, and for that reason, I want to earn your business. Please accept this gift of CUTCO and allow me to practice what I preach. This knife has been 100 percent made in America since 1949 and is guaranteed forever. Its uses are listed below, but more importantly, I want you to see the lasting value and top-of-mind awareness that this gift will bring to your clients. Thank you in advance for considering me as your marketing guru, and call me when you decide to start branding your business through CUTCO Closing Gifts.

The Spatula Spreader has a number of very cool, practical uses:

- *Spread and cut sandwiches, muffins, and rolls. Frost and cut small desserts.*
- *Slice and remove pie, brownies, lasagna, and Rice Krispies treats from pans.*
- *Spread cream cheese on bagels or butter on toast, cut tomatoes or avocados, and cut your sandwich in half.*
- *Create the perfect peanut butter and jelly sandwich!*

I genuinely appreciate you helping me build my business. I hope this piece serves your family well in the coming years, and I look forward to serving you in your business.

*In success,
Remington*

"But Remington, I'm a loan officer. I don't have knives just lying around, and I don't know what to leave behind that will have the same effect. And what do I write in the letter?"

I got you.

Here are a few ideas for small gifts that get their attention right off the bat and are worth the investment:

- **A book.** One of my favorites. You can leave a message on the inside cover that's vague or personal as to why you thought of them for this book.
- **Digital picture frame.** These are cheap and different, and you can talk about all the memories you are about to make inside and outside the business. Be careful with this one, it could get dicey.
- **Novelty candle.** These are easy to find. Pair it with the message "Smells like we are going to be working together soon." You're welcome.
- **Bottle of wine/bourbon.** Do some homework before dropping this one. Make sure it's something they like. Also, there's nothing worse than gifting a recovering alcoholic some spirits.
- **A gift for their kids.** Depending on their age, you can actually save a little money and make an even bigger splash with a gift to their kids. Dolls, trucks,

AGENT ALLIES

and toys are easy to grab and show them that you care about their family. Pair it with the message "Working with me will give you more time to spend with your loved ones."

Here's what your letter might look like with a different gift:

Dear Tracy,

Your sales and leadership in the industry have landed you on my Dream 100 List. You are someone I know I can learn from, and for that reason, I want to earn your business. Please accept this book as a token of my gratitude for how you run your business and the impact you have on those around you. I recently read this book and feel as though you would enjoy it. Here are a few reasons why:
[List said reasons.]
I genuinely appreciate your consideration in using me to help improve your business, and I look forward to seeing you at future events.

Yours truly,
[Your name]

Quick Tips:

1. Handwritten notes are more impactful.
2. Don't be too wordy. Get straight to the point.
3. Don't give this to everyone in the office. Truly make a list based on people you know you want to work with. When doing office visits, limit the amount you give out at one time.
4. Get creative with your gifting, but know that the more you streamline the process, the more likely you are to actually give out 100 gifts over the course of the year.
5. Have fun with this. I've seen a 26-pound gummy bear gifted with this strategy just to get a reaction. *It works.*

Word of Encouragement

Don't get discouraged with the process of growing clients. Celebrate the small victories. I truly believe that success at the top of the mountain feels even more amazing when you can remember the humble beginnings of starting from scratch. Create the list and let everyone know your goals. We are all goal-oriented, and helping others achieve their goals will ultimately be reciprocated.

Chapter Takeaways:

1. Be everywhere. It is more important to be in the room than to be good at your job.
2. Create your gold, silver, and bronze groups and update them often.
3. Apply the Dream 100 concept. (Read *The Ultimate Sales Machine*.)
4. Don't get discouraged. Stay the course and enjoy the journey.

CHAPTER 6

EVENT MASTERY: THE BAR IS SET LOW

When the *Real Producers* brand was created, the magazine was actually the second part of the venture. The first move was creating events.

Let's go back to when I was still selling closing gifts. I became progressively tired of all the other real estate events that were offered to me as a vendor. I was weary of sitting at a booth, for which I had paid $500 to $1,000 (sometimes more), and staring at all the other vendors who paid the same amount and, like me, were not reaching any real estate agents. And then doing it again for five other brokerages that week.

When the host booked me as a sponsor, they gave me these cards, which made me so hopeful. The organizer told us that agents would come to our table and get their cards stamped. That process was created so every single agent in attendance would come to my booth, giving me the opportunity to network and potentially sell myself and my service.

What really happened was that I would finally get one agent who was actually interested to stop and talk to me. About that time, a mad rush of agents who just had to get their card stamped would almost knock me over just to get a full card and win a pack of car washes or a wine basket. So then, not only did I miss those conversations, but the first agent was then off talking to my competitor. Yikes. Could I win the wine basket?

I was also tired of going to happy hours where only the vendors showed up. I was tired of going to the home offices of these real estate companies where only the new agents came for training and that the top producers who could afford my service were not attending. The bar was set so low that I realized if I created an event structure where I replaced all the things I did not like and pumped in more of what I did, the events would surely be a great success.

So I dipped my toes in the water amid slinging knives. My first event has been etched in history as one of the coolest success stories. It was born from the simple idea of giving away turkeys around Thanksgiving. We called it Turkey Time.

Turkey Time was an event at which we gave away a butterball turkey every 15 minutes, along with a CUTCO knife—both were free to the attendees, just for showing up. I ended up inviting my entire client database as well as anyone my clients wanted to bring. Not only did I sell a great amount of product to my current clients, but I gained a handful of new clients as well. I even included some third-party vendors to pay for the food, beverages, and turkeys as a way of sponsorship.

The success of this event sparked the idea for *Real Producers*. This event formula is one that I have duplicated many times. Since that time, for the last ten years, there has been no other third party or business that has had better attendance and praise for their events.

Pause. Hear me loud and clear on this next point: *Please stop doing events just to do them!*

The two most common mistakes I see vendors make are 1) they go to every event, regardless of whether it's worth their time, and 2) they don't have a game plan when they get there.

One of my favorite calls to host is what I call an "Event Prep Call," where I invite all of my partners to join me the day before a big event. On the call, among other things, I discuss the best ways to network and work the room at the event. This helps the salespeople avoid being "wallflowers" or the opposite, trying to talk to every single person at the event with really nothing to say other than cliché small talk.

Franco Colombu

If you're not familiar with Franco Colombu, he was a bodybuilder during the golden age alongside Arnold Schwarzenegger. Franco was a Mr. Olympian and even defeated Arnold a couple of times. He was quite literally one of the strongest men in the world.

Franco could curl well over 100 pounds and was an absolute animal in the gym. However, he often worked out with 50-pound dumbbells. One day, a man half his size who had been watching him for a couple of weeks finally broke down and approached Franco. He asked Franco why he only lifted 50-pound dumbbells.

"I can lift 50-pound dumbbells, but I don't look like you for some reason," the man said.

Franco replied, "You do not understand. My 50-pound dumbbell weighs way more than your 50-pound dumbbell."

At first, you might laugh and think to yourself, *What a head-scratcher.* When you understand what Franco was talking about, you will realize it is the core belief structure of how growth occurs.

Franco's comment revealed his strategy and technique for bodybuilding, but it can be applied to business. His one repetition was slow and very methodical, and he felt the pain of that moment and the squeeze of the movement, which became the catalyst for growth.

Some people want to lift a dumbbell as quickly as they can just to say that they lifted a heavier weight. They fail to realize that it's not just the weight of the dumbbell but the speed of the lift that matters. We have all had accidents from lifting too much or from doing a movement the wrong way. Thus, there are times in our careers when we might be just checking a box, but we are doing our businesses a disservice. It is time to start asking *how* we are doing things instead of just *why*. We know why. We want to get better. We want to grow.

Becoming an Event Specialist

The way we run an event could actually damage our businesses. The way we attend an event could also hurt our businesses more than help. Don't worry, though. Here is a basic event formula that I have created over the years that has proven to be successful in any setting. When planning an event, there are three different parts you will want to monitor: before, during, and after.

Before the Event

The time leading to the event is all about setting proper expectations and driving attendance. You accomplish this through email, social media, office visits, calling your sphere, and using partners to promote it. Ask yourself these key questions:

- Who is hosting or partnering with you on the event?
- What is everyone responsible for? What is the agenda of the event?
- What photographers and videographers will be there, and what will they be filming?
- Is there a clear social media plan?
- Are you running prep calls?
- What platforms are you using?
- Have proper expectations been laid out for the host?

- Have proper expectations been laid out for the attendees?

Setting expectations with every single person involved, including the attendees, is crucial not only for driving attendance but for getting people excited about what to expect during the event.

Remember to focus. You want to make sure you are connecting with as many people as possible but constantly moving. Your purpose is to facilitate connections. You have strategically designed every part of the event and have appointed people who have been put in a specific place and have well-defined jobs. You want to make sure that every task is properly delegated, and you must allow your people to do what they do. You are also checking in on those people, because ultimately, if they drop the ball, you drop the ball—if you know what I mean.

You want to construct a checklist that someone else will manage for the little things. (Trash cans have seemed to be the one thing that we forget constantly, so we had to put that on a checklist.) Many times, I have forgotten to eat while hosting events, which is a bummer because it's a pretty expensive lunch bill. Put it on the checklist!

During the Event

Here is the list of things that need to be monitored during the event:

- Have someone standing in a position to answer questions like "Where is the bathroom?" "Where is the food?" and "Who is Remington?"
- Encourage people at the event to post to social media. Offer a gift card to the best post or picture seen on social media.
- Push the host team to eat the food and drink the drinks so everyone else feels comfortable doing so.
- Mood setting is extremely important. Have we created the right vibe?
- Make sure the music is appropriate for the environment and loud enough to create an atmosphere.

After the Event

This is an extremely important time when you can capitalize on the excitement by getting more people engaged in your sphere and potentially even gaining more clients. Because of the FOMO effect that takes place after someone misses an event, social media should blow up. Use the pictures to send out cards and let people know they were missed. Use this as a quick opportunity to sign them up for the next one. The "What is next?" mentality should be at the forefront of your mind when you meet with someone. Always leave them with the expectation of the next time you will be seeing them.

The Hits Just Keep Coming

Here are some ideas of other events that you can do and the fun things that we have done to ensure success over the years:

- Casino Night
- Movie Night
- Sushi Party
- Costume Party
- Golf Outing
- Sand Volleyball Tournament
- Pool Party
- Ugly Sweater Party
- Taste of [Insert City]
- Wine and Paint
- Mastermind Round Table
- Euchre Tournament (for my Midwesterners)

Have some fun with this. Make it about your interests as well. One time, I became really excited about fish. Not fishing. I don't enjoy putting worms on hooks and sitting for hours waiting for something that I am going to eventually throw back in the water anyway. I am referring to aquariums. I became pumped about beautiful aquariums and had just bought one for my library. My mind was constantly swimming (yep) with ideas about the subject. At the same time, I was trying to figure out my next exciting event.

I decided to forgo a turkey giveaway at this one. Instead, I decided to give away betta fish. I know, right? It is an inexpensive option, and it is a fun marketing gimmick. Here is the payoff: one of the agents, who sells tens of millions of dollars' worth of real estate each year, won a 150-dollar chef knife and a betta fish. He came up to me a week later and said that he loved the event so much; he also gave the fish to his son and felt like a hero.

By the way, the betta fish cost me under $10, and that agent could have purchased it at any point in time. The fact that he went to an event and enjoyed the environment with people he knew and won something as little as a betta fish was the coolest thing in his mind. Stop thinking you must throw a party on a yacht and give away Rolex watches to have a successful event. Remember, the bar is set so low on the expectations of real estate functions as a whole. Loving on people, doing a couple of fun giveaways, and making it new and interesting will make your event successful. Just make sure you get the right people there.

Advice for When Things Go Wrong

Here are a few pro tips that you need to tuck away in your mind and heart:

- Things will go wrong. Have a good attitude regardless. People will feed off your energy.
- DO NOT get upset about attendance. You will end up penalizing the people who came because you are disappointed in the ones who were not in attendance. I wish I could say that I overcame this quickly. I wish.

- Roll with the punches.

Attending and hosting events is one of the greatest ways to get your name out into the real estate community and build your brand. Before hosting your own, I would recommend attending others in your market and taking mental notes of the good, the bad, and the ugly. As always, feedback is your friend. Instead of waiting for feedback on your own mistakes, ask everyone their thoughts on what makes the events awesome and build a list.

Before you know it, you will have made your own checklist and formula to become the community leader of real estate events. Practice with smaller events and work your way up. I give you permission to start with betta fish.

Chapter Takeaways:

1. Show up to events with a purpose.
2. When creating your own events, evaluate the before, during, and after game plan.
3. How you do something matters. Don't just do it to be doing it.
4. Roll with the punches and start small.

CHAPTER 7

THE STAR OF YOUR SHOW: RETHINKING YOUR MARKETING

When picking our wedding photographer, Dustin, I knew we had to get someone good. So I set a budget that I thought was generous. But then the meeting with Dustin came and it was twice what I had budgeted. But honestly, half way through I realized it was going to be totally worth it. He made us feel like we were the star of the show. The value offering was off the charts. Every conversation was about how we were going to look and how we were going to feel. I realized that this attitude can and should be duplicated in every business.

Often I find myself talking about how we can take the client to the next level because of how great we are. Now I'm not saying to ignore building of value and explaining how you are the company to do it but ask yourself, "*who is the star of your show?*" Do they feel like they are on cloud nine after your conversation? Do they feel like because of you, they will thrive?

In studying Dustin's approach and his marketing, I realized that I could be doing a better job of making my clients the star of my show. Having been in their shoes for years, it wasn't hard to nail down their pain points and tailor a marketing plan.

The Anatomy of a Winning Ad: Breaking Down the Basics

The first step is finding the medium you want to run ads on. We've already established that we want to go where the eyeballs are. Now that we know, we have to tailor an ad strategy for each medium. For most businesses, it is nearly impossible to quantify how well your marketing is doing in the first year or two.

In fact, sometimes you will get a call immediately from a medium and think, *Wow, that's how it's going to be!* It's not. Settle down. Commit to the process and realize that the compound effect is what will create a repeat client.

General rules for advertising, regardless of medium:

- **Be different/memorable:** This is actually not that hard to do. It amazes me how many people decide to put their hard-earned money into branding and fumble on the ad. Sometimes it takes weeks or even months to settle on an agreement of terms, and then people spend little to no time and effort on their ad. Or worse, they spend a ton of time, but it's just straight garbage. One big reason is it looks exactly like every other ad in the field. Big logo in the top left. A bunch of words no one will read, with a headshot in the bottom right.

- Here's the crazy thing, though. Even this is better than not doing it. Just simply getting in the game is important, and while it's boring, the consistency of it is a start. But what if you decided to flip the script and put a random animal in your ad? Keep your headshot in there but maybe even make it more of a down-to-earth photo of you in regular clothes? What if you just wrote, "Call me," with a QR code? It's different, and it can be changed next month if it doesn't land. Or better yet, build off of it for the next month. Get creative.

- **Be bold:** Stop writing a short story in your ad. No one reads that. Advertorials can be effective, but many times, the reader feels cheated when they think it's regular content and it turns out to be a sales tip. So if you are going to do an advertorial, the audience needs to know it is an advertorial going into it, *or* the sales pitch has to be subtle to nonexistent. Otherwise, people may become upset at you and the brand.
  - Bold is strong letters and colors. Sharp graphics and pictures. Big. Have your ad size represent how you view yourself in the market.
  - Why are you telling everyone you are the number one lender on the north side and then buying the smallest ad in the book? That's not

great optics. That says you think small. Work small. Build small.

- **Be clean/minimal:** My favorite ads have very little in them. They have a few words or maybe no words. They have a clear message, and they make you feel something when you see them.
- **Be funny:** *"But, Remington, I'm not funny."* Pay someone else to make your ad funny. This shows you aren't the only one in your business and you have a killer team. So what if you can't crack a joke? There are thousands of meme accounts on the internet that literally just share other people being funny—that is their content. And they have millions of followers simply because they thought of one place to put all the things they find funny and shared it with us.
- **Be clear:** Even if you follow steps 1 through 4, the ad will be lost if it does not have a clear message. How do we find you? Who is this ad for? Does it make you think about the actual product or service? Does it make you feel good or evoke a sense of urgency to call this person in the ad?

Remember to make the ad about the clients. I share two tips every renewal with my advertising partners, and rarely do they actually apply them, but when they do, it's always a big hit.

First tip: Put a real estate agent in the ad talking about why they love working with you. Remember, not all real estate agents are created equal. Just because you like working with them because they bring you business does *not* mean the real estate community is a fan. Make sure they are well-liked or, at the very least, don't have a bad reputation in the community.

You can even rotate real estate agents. Make sure you are representing different brands and that their messaging is legit. The worst thing you can do is throw an agent in your ad who you thought was cool with it, and then they go around telling people that they don't really work with you much. Yikes.

Second tip: Create your own standings with a competition attached. Use your own point system:

1. Real estate agent that sends you a deal: two points.
2. Real estate agents that refer you to other real estate agents: one point.
3. Real estate agents that post about you on social media: three points, etc.

And then throw these standings on social media and in your ad. Update it monthly and do a giveaway at the end of a period of time. Real estate agents eat this up. They love to be at the top of literally any competition you throw at them. They are salespeople! We all love that. I hope you put this book at the top of your sales books and put my name on every book standings list you make!

When we got our photos back from Dustin, we ended up spending even more money to display them everywhere. Not only was the experience of working with Dustin and his team a pure joy, not to mention load off my mind during one of the most important moments of my life, but the follow through was met with high marks as well. We talk a lot about branding and marketing in this book, but a quick reminder that eventually your product will be reviewed and it better be just as good as what your marketing suggests or it will backfire. At that point, you will hope no one has seen your ads!

Chapter Takeaways:

1. Be different/memorable.
2. Be bold.
3. Be clean/minimal (if possible; sometimes busy is good).
4. Be funny.
5. Be clear.

SECTION III

THINKING BIGGER

CHAPTER 8

THE GREATEST SALESMAN IN THE WORLD

I remember day one at my first real job in sales. Door-to-door, as they say. It wasn't really door-to-door. It was actually referral based. That would be pretty dangerous, trying to sell weapons (kitchen knives) as a 19-year-old knocking on doors. But it felt like that.

I had finally arrived. I was finally in the big-boy world with a big-boy job.

I remember my first two sales calls vividly.

The first was with the piano player at our church. She was very sweet. I was terrible. I made two unforgettable mistakes that I laugh about to this day. CUTCO had a pair of scissors that could cut through a penny. We learned the art of penny cutting in training, so I was ready. But when the time came, I choked. I couldn't cut it. I stood up and pushed down and started pumping the scissors and almost broke her table. She said, "No, really, I trust you. I'm sure it cuts pennies." I took the hint.

Then we arrived at the triumph of comparing her knife against mine. *This is where the product sells itself*, I thought. The problem was the product had apparently already sold itself in a previous appointment with a previous sales rep. She had the exact knife I was demonstrating. That didn't stop Ole Remington from following the program. I was told to read the manual. I'm a rule follower so I kept my head down and pushed forward.

She cut through the rope with one pass. "Okay…now try mine."

She took my knife and did the exact same thing.

"See, isn't that better?" I read in triumph. Needless to say, I had some skills that needed sharpening. Nonetheless, I made the sale! She bought a few knives from me to add to her collection. I drove straight home, busted down the front door, walked in the house with my chest puffed out, and said, "Mom and Dad, I'm quite literally the greatest salesman in the world." They laughed and rolled their eyes.

I couldn't bask in my glory for too long. My second appointment was already scheduled for that very same day. My aunt and uncle were two doors down. I walked over to their house, still riding high on my last kill, and did a much better presentation, it being my second time and all. I even managed to make a dent in the penny this time. To my surprise, when I got to the end of the presentation and was about to collect my dues as the greatest salesman in the world, they hit me with a "no sale" and no referrals.

Ouch! Do you even love me?

With my tail between my legs, I walked right back to the house, opened the front door, and said, "*I quit.*"

This story is 100% factual. I really did quit that day after the first bout of rejection. It hurt. I wasn't ready for that type of pain. So I was done. If not for a few hard conversations with my father about perseverance and overcoming obstacles, I might still be nursing my wounds. But I woke up the next day and made a sale and was back to GOAT status. Full disclosure, the sale was to my parents but hey, a sale is a sale!

Sales are emotional and personal. No matter what anyone says.

I do want to add that the story comes full circle with my Aunt and Uncle. Not only did they end up buying eventually, they turned out to be some of my best customers over the years to follow. We laugh about the original appointment but I honestly believe it was the best thing that could have happened to me.

Recently, I was speaking with a real estate agent who had broken the all-time record in Indiana for a year of sales; at the time, that means he surpassed 180 million sales. It's a constantly growing and ever-staggering number. He had every accolade you could imagine and had been doing it for 30 years. So I was surprised when he told me that the week before, he had lost a deal. "It was a sweet older lady, and she looked at me and said, 'I'm going with the other guy because he thinks my house is worth more.'" This is the interesting part. He said, "And that really hurt." Here was someone who could lose more deals in a year than most people make, and he was still emotional about the rejection.

This told me two things. The first is that the feelings never go away. It is normal to feel a little emotional when rejection of any kind is felt in the business world. The second is that for the elite among us, the defining factor is how long we dwell on those feelings and that situation. In time, I realized that it is okay to feel a little let down if you gave it your all and it didn't pan out. However, the ability to put that behind us and strive forward is what propels us toward success.

One of my favorite passages of Scripture is from Paul in Philippians 3. He says, *"Forgetting what lies behind and straining forward to what lies ahead... Let those of us who are mature think this way."*

This should be the mindset of everyone in the sales world. He goes on to say "I press on towards the goal..." It's much easier to focus on what went wrong but it is way more rewarding to focus on the possibility of what will happen when we strive to hit our goals.

Over time, I was able to mature as a player in the sales world. I became less emotional about each individual appointment and more focused on what I could control in the moment and how hard I worked. I still bust down my parents' door from time to time to remind them how great of a salesman I am. After all, they are my biggest fans. They are also my biggest customers, as my mother reminds me every time I get a big head.

A great way to keep your emotions in check is to fully book your day and not allow room for idol time. Idol time breeds negativity. Keeping your schedule full quite literally doesn't allow any time for negativity. If I have six appointments lined up for the day, and one or two go poorly or get canceled, I'm moving on to the next appointment with no time to think about the negative aspects. But if I have an appointment at 10am on a Tuesday, and my next appointment isn't until 4pm the next day, then I have a solid day to dwell on how that *one* appointment went. Chances are, it wasn't the result I wanted and now my whole week is being uprooted because of one appointment and poor scheduling.

This business is emotional. However, the ones who look like they have mastered the game are simply better with their time. It's like my good buddy and St. Louis *Real Producers* franchise owner, Nick Najjar always says, "*Don't let emotions dictate the logic of the situation.*" Nick was one of the fastest franchise launches in Real Producers history. He knows a thing or two. If something negative happens, he addresses it and moves on.

For instance, if you feel like you have been on the phone all day and don't have anything to show for it, it would be easy to get frustrated and feel like you are working hard with no results. When logic steps in, you realize that you only made a fraction of the calls you set out to make and really you should be more intentional with the number of calls you made and less emotional about the results of a few rejections.

If emotions and belief is something you struggle with, visit remingtonramsey.com. I have a free ebook I would like to give you entitled *Belief is Rooted in Truth*. Emotions seem to impact those with less faith and the ebook has practical advice on how to attack it head on with lessons learned from the animal kingdom. It's a short read and a good reset for the mind.

Chapter Takeaways:

1. Sales are emotional. The important distinction is how long you dwell on negative emotions.
2. Maturity is forgetting what is behind and pressing on towards the goal.
3. Don't let emotions dictate the logic of your situation.
4. Download my free ebook, *Belief is Rooted in Truth* at remingtonramsey.com.

CHAPTER 9

BECOMING RECESSION-PROOF

Growing up, my favorite place in the world was on the lake. I loved everything about it. I loved the smell; I loved swimming, boating, skiing; and I even loved getting slightly sunburned because it was a reminder that I had been at the lake. So, the second I started putting money away after buying my first home, I knew my first investment had to be a lake house.

When I finally raised enough capital to buy a second home, I traveled to northern Indiana, where my family had owned a lake house for 60 years. After the usual real estate adventure of looking, offering, countering, losing, looking, and finally landing, I wound up purchasing a house. In reality, it was not a house at all but a shack—less than 600 square feet of lake paradise that was barely standing up.

> **SIDENOTE:** It is never required that you begin big. Getting into the game as soon as possible is the key.

I made a down payment and immediately started dreaming of plans to radically change our family's summers and the future lives of our children. Not that I recommend my strategy, but we bought it "sight unseen," at least on the inside. I just wanted the lot and was prepared to knock the house down if it turned out to be condemned. After our inspection, the bones of the home were good, and really, all it needed was a little bit of TLC and a coat of paint. We could not resist calling it *"The Shack"*, a name it retains even today.

At some point, I had an epiphany. I was going to own The Shack regardless of how much money it could generate, but if I could make money on the side to pay for this summer vacation home, then it would truly be what lifestyle investing is all about. I had wanted to test the waters with a short-term rental business. So I listed The Shack as a rental on weekends when we weren't going up to the lake. In the first summer, it generated around $10,000, which was half of what it cost to run this second home.

Then I realized that there was money to be made in the off-season because I had no intention of staying there when the lake was frozen and there was snow on the ground. I am more of a "fun-in-the-sun" kind of guy, and the lake frontage along with my boats, docks, and extra-large lot had the makings of some classic lake life. The off-season was fair game for income potential.

AGENT ALLIES

This was my entrance into the world of owning real estate and investing in properties as a side hustle. As I mentioned, a single real estate deal feeds a lot of families. There are so many businesses involved in the sale of a single home. In most transactions, the buyers and sellers are represented by different agents. Two-thirds of the homes in America have mortgages. Every real estate deal has title work, and some even have title attorneys. Most, if not all, of the homes have had a home inspection prior to the finalization of the home sale.

Are you doing the math? We have listed six potential individuals who get a piece of the large pie representing the sale of a home. Now just think about getting a house ready to be sold. Most of the time, a home needs some work to get it into top shape and ready to be listed on the market. Painters and handymen are on speed dial. Photographers and even videographers are called upon to make the listing pop. Cleaning companies come in and do one last sweep. Moving and junk removal companies rid the property of any remaining items that would detract from the curb appeal both inside and out, and in the final stretch, the process is brought to completion.

While this is happening, across town, in another city or state, the sellers are most likely—you guessed it—working on another home that more than likely had the same amount of people doing the same tasks to their new and exciting home. There are also some other honorable mentions on this home acquisition team:

- Landscapers
- Plumbers

- Roofers
- Home builders
- Home warranty companies
- Interior decorating designers
- Restoration specialists
- HVAC (heating and air-conditioning)
- Flooring companies
- Pest control businesses

And the list goes on.

Now that we have established all the players involved in a real estate deal, it is important to explore the four reasons why people connected to this industry should own real estate. My point is that if you are going to spend so much time in the arena, you might as well get in the game yourself.

What Should You Do?

First, these professionals have insider knowledge of what to look for in a quality property.

Second, they have a business that can help land a good deal with expertise.

Third, they have connections, and if they are doing it the right way, they have the advantage of making the transaction less expensive with a seamless process.

Fourth, they have access to properties before the masses do.

Why is real estate a sound investment? If you do a quick Google search of the history of all the billionaires who have ever lived, it won't take long to conclude the one thing they all have in common.

Whether it is growing their wealth or securing their wealth, real estate is the most popular choice. Why?

I can think of four big reasons:

1. Passive cash flow
2. Appreciation of assets
3. Tax benefits
4. Options

During the pandemic, I pivoted to doing weekly Zoom masterclass calls until we knew what the new normal would bring. Some of the best content came out of those six weeks. My absolute favorite panel that still gets requested to this day involved three real estate agents, each with a completely different strategy and rental portfolio. I asked questions and picked apart their thinking. They explained how they maximize their revenue, and it was eye-opening. It showed me that there really is more than one way to skin a cat. What a great phrase for a truly overrated animal.

One focused on all long term rentals and didn't care about cash flow as much as the long term benefit of equity. Another invested in short term rentals and wanted as many doors as possible to bring in cash flow for more deals. The third was focused solely on luxury short term and charged upwards of 4 figures a night.

Real estate is the centerpiece of our economy, and the people involved in every aspect of the sale would be foolish to not use their knowledge to invest. Also, it is the best way to be recession-proof. Everyone thinks they know what industries or even businesses are recession-proof. We could list liquor stores, plumbers, and food industries, and to be honest, all of those could have a place in the standings of the most recession-proof businesses.

However, without a doubt, the most recession-proof business is one that is leveraged with other businesses (so go ahead and start that side hustle). As a serial entrepreneur, of course, I would be expected to have this stance. But I believe real estate agents have the best opportunity when it comes to investing in property. They get so focused on that next sale that they don't realize that one of the best opportunities they have has nothing to do with representing a buyer or seller.

Here are some great options:

- Flipping homes
- Long-term rentals
- Short-term rentals
- Commercial property
- Land hacking
- Mobile home park investing
- Recruiting
- Coaching and training
- Social media content and/or design
- Residential assisted living

And the list goes on...

This advantage does not just apply to real estate agents but to everyone in the real estate community. Loan officers, home inspectors, and everyone connected to real estate should have side hustles. You have all this knowledge. Use it. Who gets rich in a gold rush? It isn't most of the gold diggers; it's the guy selling shovels! I share this only to remind you that there is plenty of money to be made in the industry outside of the buying and selling of homes. The largest trade organization in the world is made up of agents, and they need their shovels. I am going to continue selling shovels, buckets, water, and anything else to support the cause.

Agents are brought into one of the tightest niche communities any city has to offer. Within their brokerages exists a pool of leads (other real estate agents) who can either buy what you are selling or get you in front of an even deeper pool of leads (their clients) and give you ideas of side hustles that can be amplified by all the agents you know. Talk about *Agent Allies*! What an opportunity!

Some examples include the following:

- Photography
- Videography
- Staging
- Junk removal
- Closing gifts
- Handyman service
- Remote notary
- Professional showing agent
- Administration support
- Cleaning and organizing

Do I need to say the list goes on?

Moving companies are among the most fascinating to me. For the most part, the entire industry still believes in mass marketing. Not that it does not work, but for me, I want to go directly to the source. NAR states that 87 percent of homebuyers use an agent and 90 percent of sellers use an agent. Ladies and gentlemen, we have found the source. Instead of throwing up a billboard or spending hundreds of thousands on commercials, why not invest a fraction of that in reaching real estate agents? Everyone they work with is literally moving! I digress.

My dream of owning a lakehouse first came to life during those early days in the local real estate offices. After giving my 6 minute closing gift presentation, I sat in the back of sales meetings and just listened in. That was how my passion really started to develop. It seemed so simple and I really couldn't believe the amount of real estate professionals that didn't take advantage of their knowledge and decide to invest. I truly feel blessed to have jumped in early so that my family could not only enjoy the time spent at the lake, but also be growing equity should the need for money ever arise.

Chapter Takeaways:

1. The most recession proof business is one that is leveraged by other businesses
2. Side hustles should remain side hustles until they are not
3. Real estate agents have a big advantage to starting a side hustle that supports their business

CHAPTER 10

IT'S ALL ABOUT THE STORY

Storytelling has been a central theme, not only in this book but at the core of everything I have ever done. Stories are relatable and thought provoking. They stir up emotions and create connections. Powerful stories can increase value or even destroy it. Sharing your story builds connections and connections build the business.

Just to fully demonstrate my point, here's one more story.

I'll never forget the first time Grandpa took me to a professional baseball game. We drove from Muncie, Indiana, down to Cincinnati to watch the Reds and naturally had to stop at Skyline Chili on the way. After scarfing down three, maybe four chili dogs, we walked into the stadium and it was electric. To this day, the smell of light beer still takes me back to this memory as it was the first time I had ever smelled it. Wasn't a fan, but I was a fan of the cotton candy.

The highlight of this memory came midway through the game, when Benito Santiago hit a foul ball that was caught by one of my grandpa's friends. He immediately turned around, said, "Here you go, kid," and tossed it to me. I'm not a huge baseball fan these days. I can really only name the players that I heard talked about as Hall of Famers, but I will *never* forget the name Benito Santiago because of that baseball.

Millions of baseballs are sold every year, and a quick Google search tells me that it costs less than fifty cents to produce a single baseball on average. We purchase them for between seven and ten dollars at most sporting goods stores. Why, then, do some baseballs sell for millions of dollars?

It's all about the story.

One of the most exciting seasons in Major League Baseball history was in 1998, when Sammy Sosa and Mark McGwire faced off in a home run duel to break the record for single-season home runs. The record to beat was 61 home runs, a record that was set by Roger Maris in 1961. They both ended up breaking the record, and Mark McGwire reigned victorious at the end of the season with 70 home runs.

A buddy of mine is a huge St. Louis Cardinals fan and went to many home games that season. He told me about his friend who caught the 63rd home run hit by Mark McGwire. The club said it could be worth up to $500,000 at that moment. He held out. Someone offered him $150,000 a few days later, and he took it. Why? Because McGwire still had a few games left that season, and every home run hit after the 63rd would bring the value of the ball down. The real value was in the final home run ball hit to set the record.

AGENT ALLIES

Isn't it amazing how two baseballs made on an assembly line for fifty cents each can have completely different values a week later? If I set my Benito Santiago foul ball next to the 63rd home run ball hit by Mark McGwire, it's possible that you couldn't tell the difference. That's because, from a manufacturing point of view, there is literally no difference. However, one is worth hundreds of thousands, while the other is worth virtually nothing...except to me. I'm sure you have items like this too. Most people do.

Like I said, it's all about the story.

When you think about the value you bring to the table, you should be thinking about your story. What is the impact you are having on the world around you? Are you currently living the story you would be excited to write about?

There was a time where I didn't see myself venturing off from selling closing gifts. Life was good and I was comfortable. Had I not jumped into the world of entrepreneurship, I wouldn't have been living up to my potential and I would have deprived the world of all the good that *Real Producers* has provided. Top agents from all over the country talk about the impact that *Real Producers* has had with connecting the best real estate professionals and strengthening the community.

There is a chance I still would've written *Agent Allies* because of the lessons I learned in building that first business but it would be missing all that I have learned in the last 10 years of building, recruiting and coaching the best in the industry.

The beauty of this world is that you can work on changing the narrative at any moment. Remember that everyone loves a good story. A good story can change the value of a painting, a book, or even a pair of pants. I recently came across a company that makes specialty mugs carved out of baseball bats. It was founded by an ex-MLB player, and the story causes people to pay more for these mugs than they would for a mug carved out of any ordinary piece of wood.

The point I really want to drive home is that you are in control of your own narrative and it's possible to become the story you see in your head. When I first started selling knives, people thought it was goofy and really not all that different from a little leaguer selling chocolate door to door. But when I worked hard and silenced the critics, over time everyone saw me as a serious businessman and the narrative changed. There is someone in real estate reading this right now that needs a shot in the arm. You are not living up to your potential and you have bought into the mediocre story of your own life. Silence the critics and do things that may get laughed at. Skip the parties and work hard when everyone else is slacking. Make the sacrifices and build the story of your life that is truly great.

That foul ball I have is worth way more to me than it is to anyone else. The story is what matters to me, and to my knowledge, no one else has a story to compete that makes it more valuable to them. This is a true testament to scalability. How many more people want that home run ball? You have to determine who your audience is and then figure out what makes them tick. Get involved in the community and give them something to write about. Be the best at what you do so that something you touch or leave an impact on is worth more than it was before.

AGENT ALLIES

A legendary entrepreneur once told me, "*They never write your net worth on your tombstone.*" When I asked him what he wanted to be remembered for his answer was quick. "Integrity". Hard to argue with that. What would your answer be? Your story is still being written as is mine.

There is no shame in being worth a lot to one person, just like the Benito Santiago ball. But if I know my readership, the goal is to have a lasting impact on as many people as possible. So work on your game and swing for the fences. Maybe one day, people will be fighting over your home run ball.

PAY IT FORWARD

A few years ago, I started a new reading tradition of reading 24 books a year (2 books a month). It's a great goal to have. I have found that most people I run into struggle to hit their reading goals so I am always prompted to give them a book to spark their new habit of reading regularly.

I also realized that gifting can get rather expensive in the business world, especially if you are doing it for all your clients.

But I wasn't always in a place where I could spend $100-plus on all of my clients, so I started gifting books that I had read. It's way less expensive and oftentimes even more impactful.

Now, any time I buy a book, I try to buy two copies so I can read one and give the other as a gift. You can have a friend to hold you accountable in the read, *and* it's a thoughtful gesture. I was looking around in my library one day and couldn't find any of the books I had read, and I realized that I had gifted the others as well.

Now, that's what I do with most books. As soon as I'm done reading them, I give them away with a handwritten note explaining why I thought of that person. A word of encouragement. It never fails to bring a smile and appreciation. I would encourage you to try it with this book. You don't need it. You already read it. Your friend needs it. And if you want to read it again later, you can find it wherever books are sold. Cheers.